Refinement Time

30-day Inspirational Journal
of God's Love to Being Made Better

Randi Coley

Refined Community Outreach
Chicago, Illinois

This is a work of Nonfiction. It is an inspirational book. All parts of this work are concepts from the author's podcast- Refinement Time on Anchor, found on Spotify. Refinement Time by Randi Coley

Publishing under RCO-Refined Real Talk Community Outreach Copyright 2023

ISBN Paperwork- 978-1-359060-00-0
ISBN eBook- 978-1-959060-01-7

All scripture quotations are from The Thompson Chain -Reference Bible (KJV) fifth improved edition copyright 1908,1917. 1929, 1934, 1957, 1964, 1982, and 1988. All rights reserved throughout the world. 22nd printing July 2018 entered at Stationers Hall, London

Cover designed by: J. L Woodson www.jlwoodson.com
Interior design by: Naleighnia Kai

Cover Image: Woodson Creative Studio
www.woodsoncreativestudio.com

Printed in the United States of America

Dedication

To the women in my family who came before me. My mother Beverly Coley that raised me. My grandmothers Lois Swinney and Cordelia Kizer that were my friends, and stern examples of womanhood.

To my daughters Jordan and Toriann the future is limitless.

To Jesse Hoover, the first man to tell me and show me what being valued was. My dad, I miss you.

To Isadore Kizer, my father- Losing you surprised me, and made me know the Grace of God is real. I miss you, old man.

Acknowledgements

I give all praise and honor to the Almighty Sovereign Lord God for the grace that allows me to use the talent(s), and gifts he has given to me.

To my brothers and sisters in the body of Christ who encourage and uplift me day to day. To my daughters Jordan and Toriann because without you, I would have never done this. You encouraged me and waited with expectation for me to complete the writing of my thoughts.

To everyone I have mentioned, and anyone I have forgotten, thank you for everything.

I pray God's continued blessings on your life.

Table of Contents

Emotional Topics:

Mental Health Topics

Physical Topics

Spiritual Topics

Introduction

In 2006, after a trial of my faith, God began to deal with my heart, and guide me toward his word, his way for me to live, and love. It was not the love of a "man", or humankind. It was his eternal, Godly love. In the beginning, I called it a "Journey into Love". As time went on, at the next phase I called it "Grandmother's Chronicles". I now call it "Refinement Time." All three are different names which all take me to and are references for the same thing. The references for being made better. I know it can make me whole through my life in God. In his love, and through the guidance of his word. As a licensed counselor, I have added a touch of Psycho-Social tips to apply after each of the lessons as an example.

Statements regarding love:

1. Love is the unconscious desire that leads to a deliberate decision to respect, adore and give honor to those we pledge ourselves to by blood or in bond. Please refer to Romans 12:10.

2. The power of love is so powerful, it will show you, and teach you, how to exhibit the actions of love purely.
 Please refer to 1.Corinthians 13:13

 3. Agape (Ancient Greek ἀγάπη, agapē) is a Greco-Christian term referring to love, "the highest form of love, charity" and "the love of God for man and of man for God". The word id not to be confused with philia, which is brotherly love, or philauria which is self-love. Agape is the unconditional love that transcends and persists regardless of circumstance. Please refer to John. 3:16-17

Many people deal with life in terms of self-love, that has no part of what I am talking about. I am talking in terms of love and humanitarianism on a whole different scope. What I am talking about is love that can only be the true long-suffering love of God. The only way of doing this is to be made better. It's refinement time.

Devotional Notes to Reader

In putting this devotional together, with consideration of how to best help the person reading this. It is my prayer, and hope that you would receive the most out of the time you engage with this 30-day journal. The very goal is to feel the touch of God's love, his many attributes, and his desires for us. It is my hope that you would use this devotional as an experience to grow in a relationship with God.

I have found several points to help, and they are:
To be fully engaged in this change of love process, the major help has always been journaling through the learning process to reflect.:

1. You will need the love journal with a pen or pencil to write with.

2. Get to a quiet place to connect with God's love.

3. When you awaken in the morning, pray, read the word of GOD, then quiet your mind and open your heart to receive God's love.

4. Release all preconceived notions of how loving kindness should unfold to you
.

5. Be present, tune in and let love come ny way that it wants to be shared with you.

6. Once you recognize God's loving kindness, write the words of love in your journal and what God's love speaks to you. Allow yourself to meditate on it throughout the day.

7. Engage in this practice every day and he will speak his loving way to change to you.

Let's do this!!!

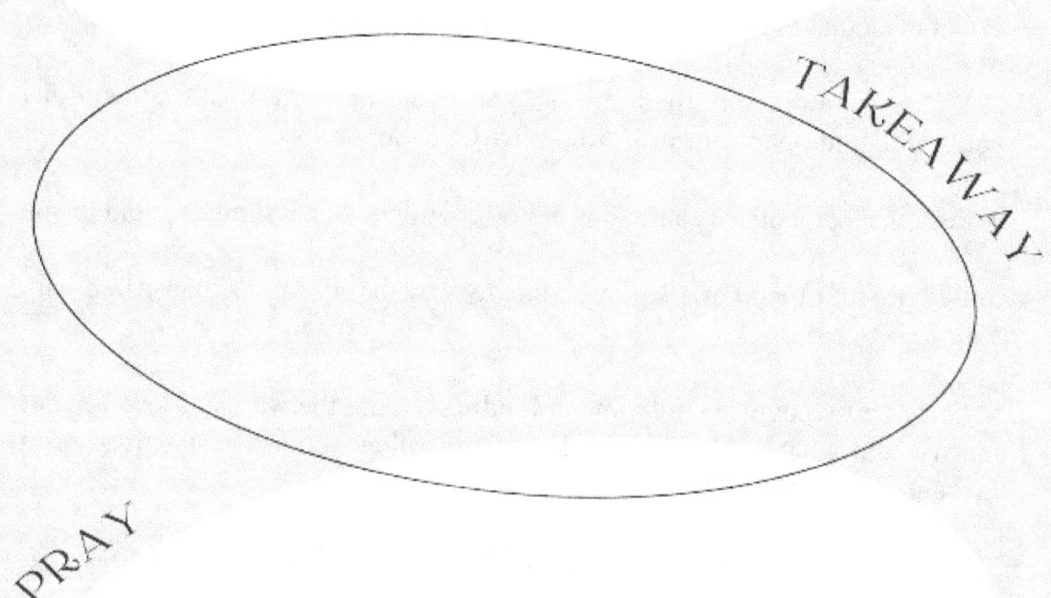

REVIEW

TAKEAWAY

PRAY

Part One
Emotional Refinement:

"He healeth the broken in heart, and bindeth up their wounds."
Psalms 147:3 KJV

Day 1

ANGER

Indignation/rage or wrath. Is the definition of anger.

Ephesians. 4:26 "Be ye angry, and sin not: let not the sun go down upon your wrath:"

As a younger woman, I had a volatile temper. I was quiet and withdrawn. However, if I became angry at someone, "I would act the fool". I was the woman that would bust the windows out the car. I know now that those responses were over the top. In reflection, it was due to responding without self-awareness or emotional maturity. God's love has addressed me and is teaching me to be more self-aware of my response in anger. Now, I just allow God's love to work through me. I have learned to quiet myself, take a deep breath, and let go.

Three tips:

1.   Don't speak in anger.
2.   Step back and allow your emotions to cool down.
3.   Listen to music, read, or pray.

How do you deal with anger?

_____

_____

_____

_____

_____

_____

_____

_____

_____

_____

_____

_____

PROCESS

REVIEW

TAKEAWAY

PRAY

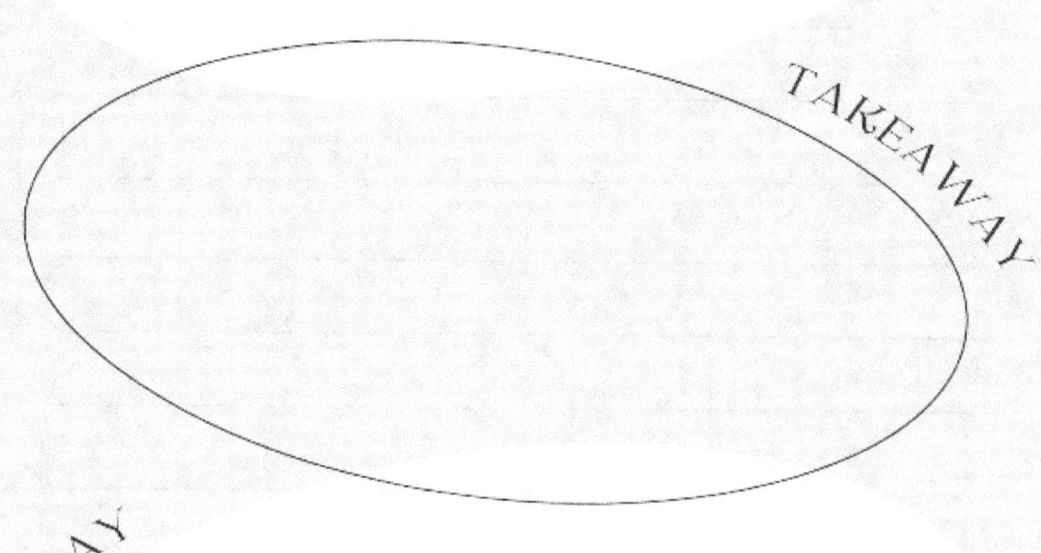

Day 2

HATING

Since the popularity of social media, there is an increase in a term called hating, which comes from the slang term hater. The definition is, as an individual who talks or behaves negatively in response to another's success goals and achievement.
 Psalms 119:42 "So shall I have wherewith to answer him that reproacheth me: for I trust in thy word."

One thing I have learned as time has gone on, "hating" is not what many believe it to be. When someone has displeasure in you, they respond in ways that are unkind. Now, as I have gained knowledge, I see the term "hating" is not what many believe it to be. People that "are hating on you" follow you on social media, they mimic you, they learn from the things you do. You are an influencer. Use it to your advantage.

Three tips:

1.   Be authentic- no gimmicks.
2.   Let your personality shine.
3.   Don't take criticism to heart.

Learn that all criticism is beneficial even when it hurts.

How do you use your personality to show love, help others?

_____

_____

_____

_____

_____

_____

_____

_____

_____

_____

_____

_____

REFINEMENT REVIEW
PROCESS

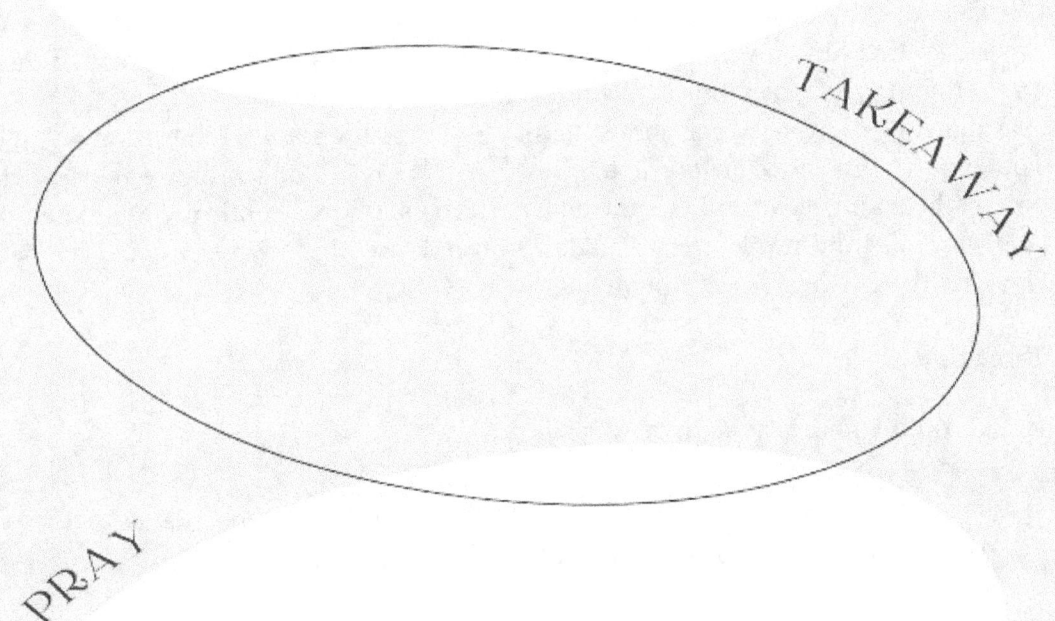

REVIEW

TAKEAWAY

PRAY

Day 3

FEAR

Fear is as an intense, often potent emotion caused by the expectation or awareness of fear.

Isaiah. 43: 1-5 (Isaiah.43:5)

In October 1993, I suffered a violent assault. Also, there were some trying times with friendships, relationships, and mental health. After the assault, developed a fear of dying and a general fear of living after the assault. At some point I had a dream of what I believed was the judgement of God. The dream was scary. A few months later, I had an experience that can only be God's lovingkindness. It was as if someone wrapped their arms around me in an embrace to comfort me.

Fear didn't go away, however, someone that I wronged sent me a letter forgiving me. The Scripture included in the letter was Isaiah 43:1-5. God's promise to Israel to protect them and keep them safe through hard trials. It was a confirmation to me that God was real. I did not lose fear. I did, however, know that whatever could happen. God was there to bring me through it.

Three tips:

1. Think of the fear you have, reflect on it.
2. Face your fear.
3. Go into your bible and look under the word fear in the concordance. There are at least 100 entries that tell you not to fear.

What helps you to move away from fear?

_____

_____

_____

_____

_____

_____

_____

_____

_____

_____

_____

_____

_____

REFINEMENT REVIEW
PROCESS

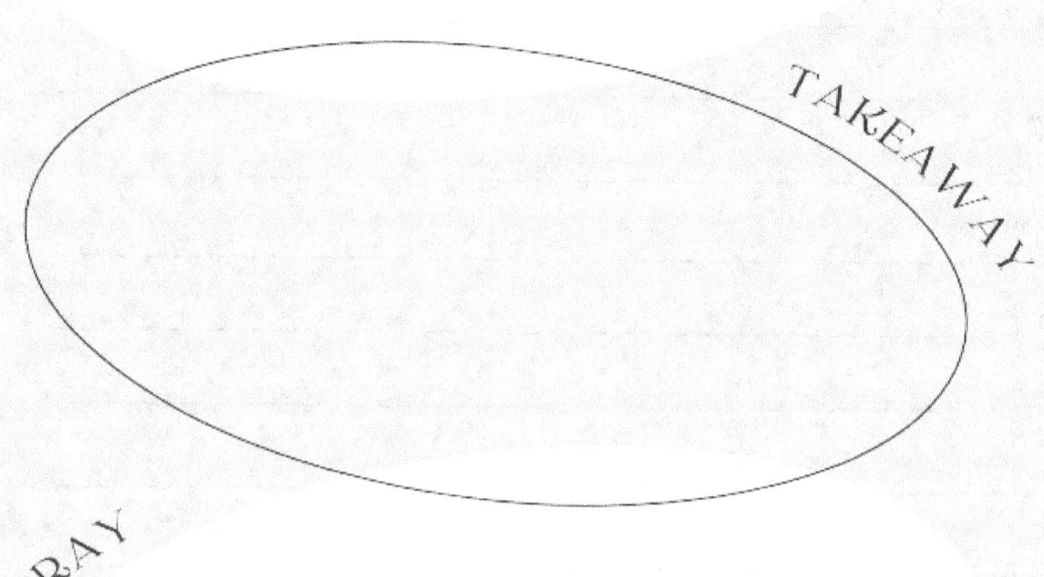

REVIEW

TAKEAWAY

PRAY

Day 4

JOY

Feeling of great pleasure and happiness is Joy defined.

Ecclesiastes 11:9 God will bring thee into Joy.

There are moments when life becomes difficult , and you may not feel happy. For many years, I suffered from clinical depression. It was in experiencing God's love that I learned to feel joy. In the movie The Bucket List, there is a conversation with the question "Have you found the joy in your life?" Once you have found joy in your life, nothing can ever take it away.

Three tips:
1.   Do something you enjoy.
2.   Laugh
3.   Listen to music, read or watch something that lifts your spirits.

Have you found joy? What brings you joy

_____

_____

_____

_____

_____

_____

_____

_____

_____

_____

_____

_____

_____

_____

REVIEW

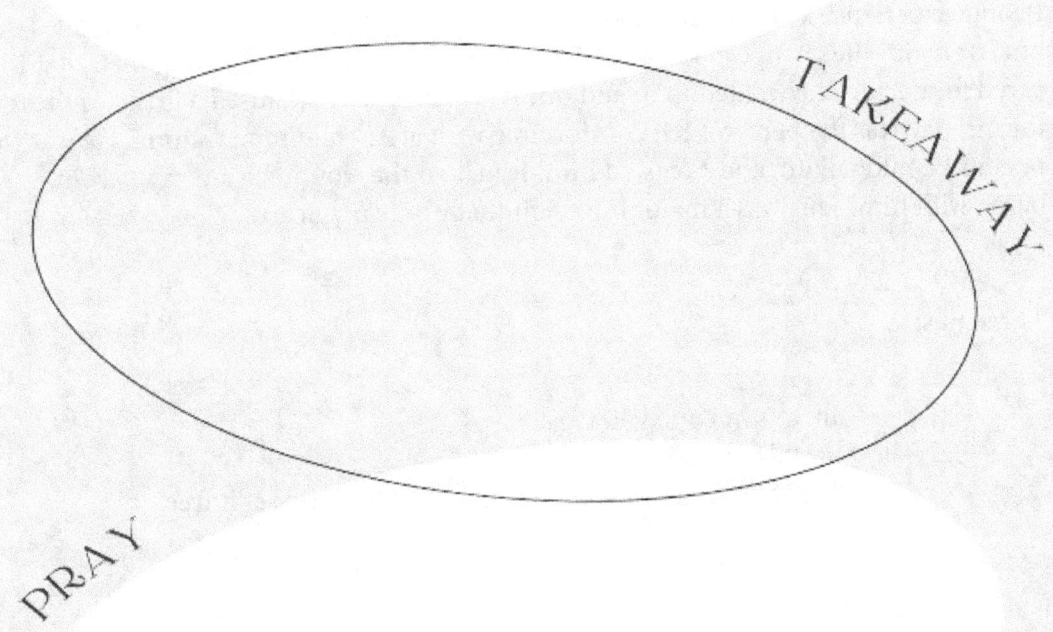

TAKEAWAY

PRAY

Day 5

SADNESS

Sadness is being as affected with unhappiness.

Ecclesiastes. 7:3- "Sorrow is better than laughter: for by the sadness of the countenance, the heart is made better."

People experience sadness after a loss, such as a broken heart, the death of a loved one, or major life change. Soon after, I gave birth to my son. The young man that I cared for decided he wanted to to end our relationship. This caused a great sadness for me. He was the person I felt comfortable with after childhood trauma. He was the person I could talk to, and I trusted him. It helped the wounds from my past in being with him. This was a major life event that broke my heart.

Three tips:

1.   Talk to someone you trust.
2.   Journal your feelings.
3.   Give yourself a timeline to release sadness and set it free.

What has sadness taught you?

_____

_____

_____

_____

_____

_____

_____

_____

_____

_____

_____

_____

_____

REFINEMENT REVIEW
PROCESS

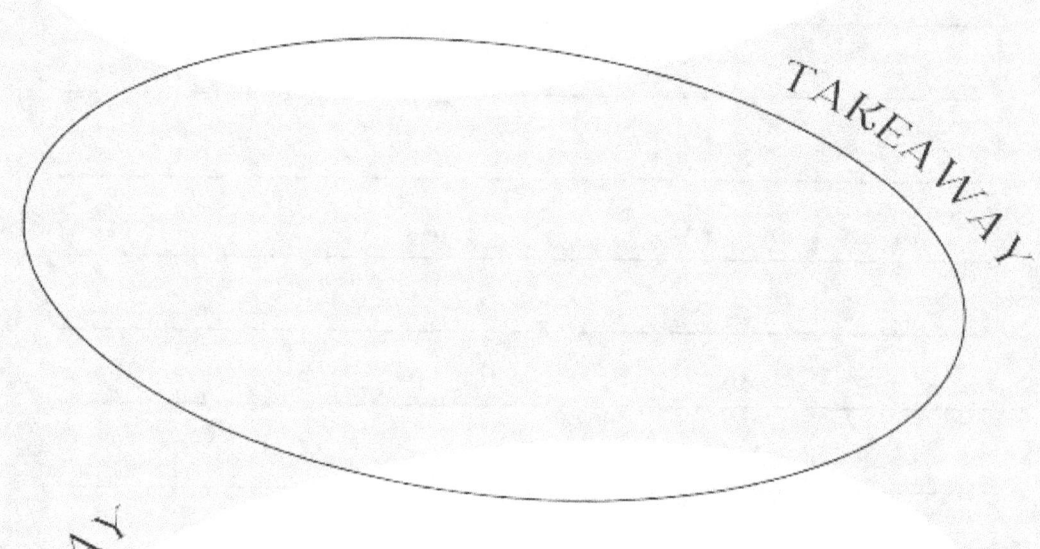

REVIEW

TAKEAWAY

PRAY

Day 6

LOVE

Love is an attachment, enthusiasm or devotion, or admiration to.

John.3:16-17"For God so loved the world, that he gave his only begotten Son, that whosoever believeth in him should not perish, but have everlasting life. For God sent not his Son into the world to condemn the world; but that the world through him might be saved."
Love causes no losses. It is pure without suspicion, and never let's go. Love can change yet, it does not diminish. Whether we speak or pass one another without a word. My love does not go away.

When I say I love you, that does not change. My devotion remains. Part of the ways I show love are acts of service, words of affirmation, and gift giving. I always remember the love. Our connection can end, my feeling remain and from time to time that ache reminds me of you. Depending on the level of the separation, we may stay in touch, we may not. I always pray for you. Love has changed me in that way.

Three tips:

1. Speak only in love.
2. Allow love to move emotionally before you do physically.
3. Study what love is, true love, godly love, and pray for guidance in love.

How has love changed for you?

_____

_____

_____

_____

_____

_____

_____

_____

_____

_____

_____

_____

_____

PROCESS

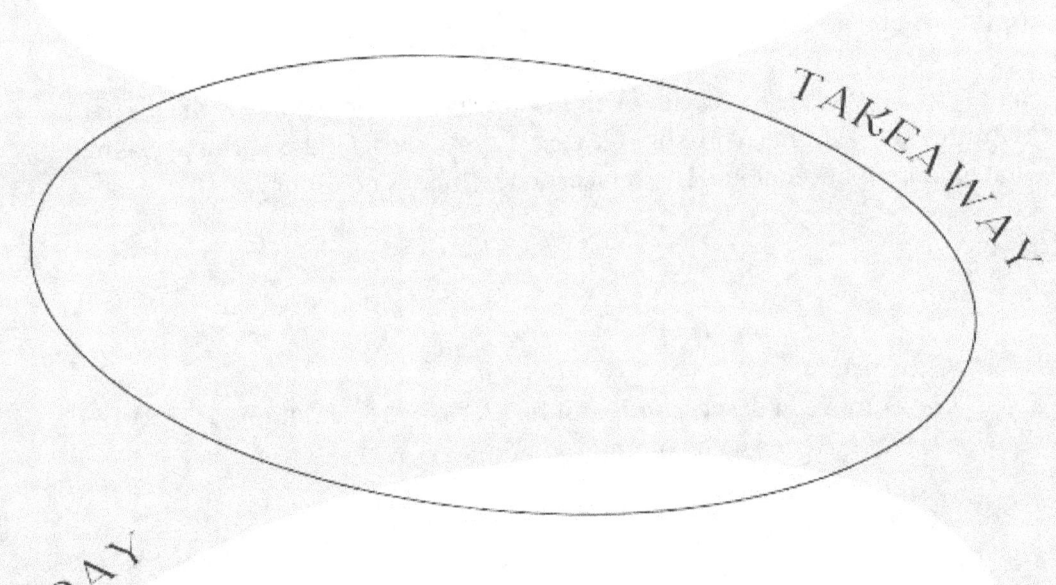

REVIEW

TAKEAWAY

PRAY

Day 7

LONELY

Sadness is from being alone, is the definition of lonely. There are times I feel like I am chasing love. Loneliness is a part of life's existence. Most don't comprehend loneliness. After my long-term relationship ended, I was very lonely.

Because I chose not to date.. There were a lot of instances when the desire for companionship and someone to spend time with was so overwhelming. It was like the desire to scratch. No matter what, I could not abate the feeling. Eventually, I met people who had the same interests, and I got a dog to keep me company. One evening in prayer, I heard the scripture that is printed below.

Hebrews 13:5c For he hath said, I will never leave thee, nor forsake thee. That scripture stays with me, and I hold it close to my heart. God is with me no matter what, and I am never alone. Lesson learned- Alone is not lonely.

Three tips:

1.   Get a pet.
2.   Never move in desperation, wait for clarity when emotions are involved.
3.   Seek out friends with common interests.

How do you face loneliness? Do you deal with it, or do you try to suppress it?

_____

_____

_____

_____

_____

_____

_____

_____

_____

_____

_____

_____

_____

REFINEMENT REVIEW
PROCESS

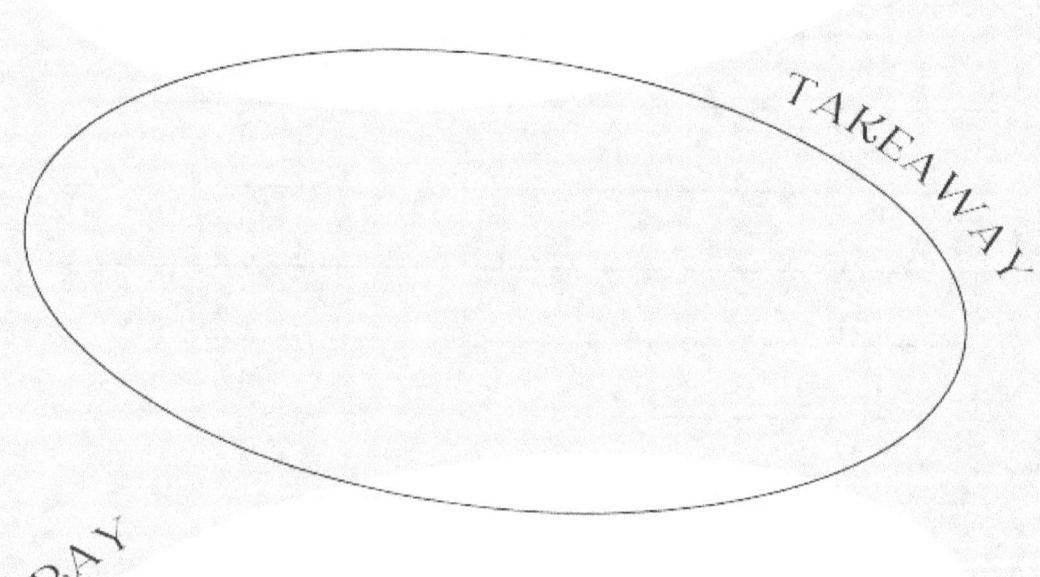

REVIEW

TAKEAWAY

PRAY

Part Two
Mental Refinement:

"Again, they are minished and brought low through oppression, affliction, and sorrow."--Psalms 107:39 KJV

Day 8

ANXIETY

For most of my life, anxiety has plagued me. That feeling of apprehension, uneasiness, or nervousness usually over an impending or anticipated ill.

Most people have been through some form of trauma or situation that can cause them to be apprehensive or careful. I liken my life to the children's book "A Series of Unfortunate Events" with lots of traumas and misuse. It wasn't all bad, just like everyone I have scars. Mine were emotional and mental scars. I have affected a lot of people in the past. I have spent a lot of time learning ways to overcome anxiety and with the help of God, I am adept at spotting the beginning signs of anxiety. This gives balance back to my daily functioning.

As my faith and love in God increases, I find he has given me strategies to ease anxiety for me.

Philippians.4:6 "Be careful for nothing; but in everything by prayer and supplication with thanksgiving, let your requests be made known unto God". See 1Peter.5:7.

Five tips
1. Close your eyes, take slow deep breaths.
2. Control your thoughts, think positive.
3. Exercise regularly.
4. Talk when needed (spend time with others.
5. Do something you enjoy.

How do you deal with anxiety?

_____

_____

_____

_____

_____

_____

_____

_____

_____

_____

_____

_____

_____

PROCESS

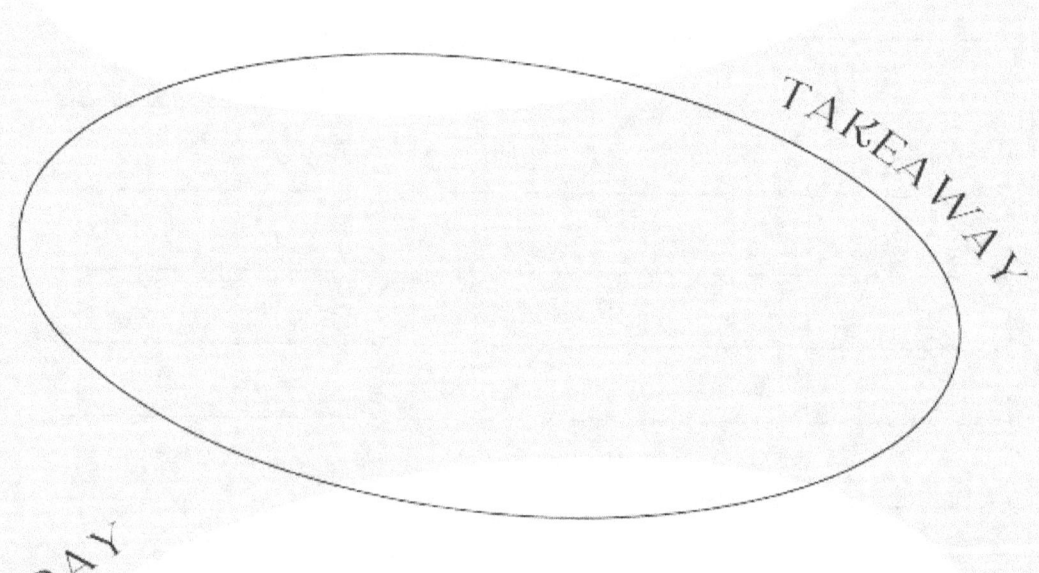

REVIEW

TAKEAWAY

PRAY

Day 9

BURNOUT

In 2020, after several baffling rough months in quarantine. I experienced an exhaustion that stole all of my physical and emotional strength. It caused my motivation to dwindle. Which the doctor said was usually a result of prolonged stress and or frustration. I was in a full bout of burnout.

My daughter had just come home the year before. After being incarcerated for three years. All the while I had custody of her two young children that had recently turned 4 and 3. My mother contracted Covid and was bedridden. I was working days and taking care of her at night. Two of my cousins dies, and four long-time friends. During those trying weeks, I suffered a medical crisis. Giving up crossed my mind. The scripture below helped me through it. I learned to make myself wait for a change and quiet my heart through all the chaos.

Isaiah 40:31- But they that wait upon the Lord shall renew their strength; they shall mount up with wings as eagles; they shall run and not be weary; and they shall walk and not faint.

At time life is full. Covid quarantine taught me to relax, and take care of myself.

Three tips:

1. Pay attention to your body.
2. Get adequate sleep, 6.5-9 hours a night.
3. Say No.

When you are weary (tired), stressed, or lack motivation, what do you do to renew yourself?

_____

_____

_____

_____

_____

_____

_____

_____

_____

_____

_____

_____

_____

PROCESS

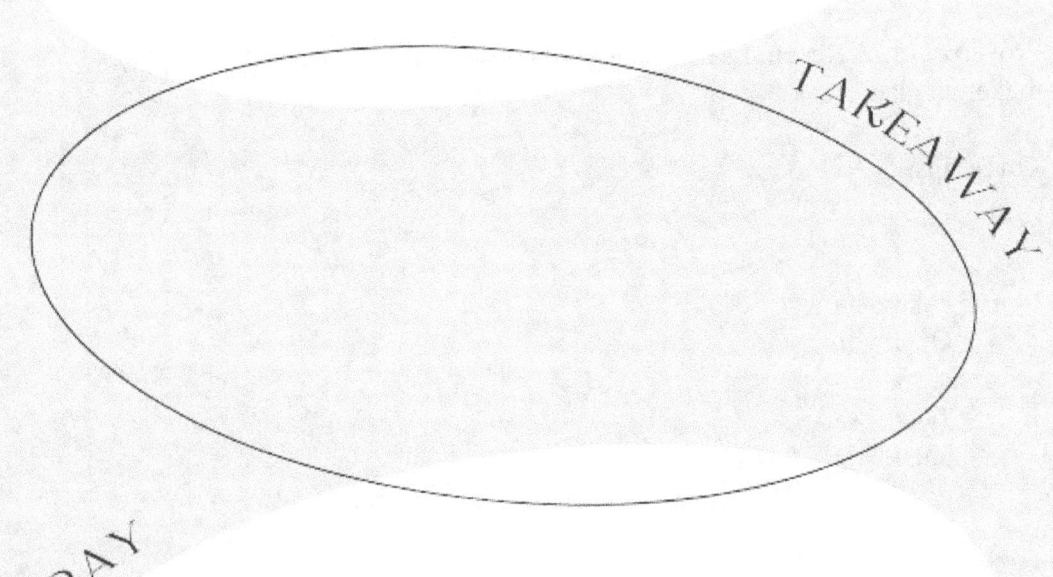

REVIEW

TAKEAWAY

PRAY

Day 10

DEPRESSION

Melancholy is a state of feeling sad. Or when you are feeling down in a low spirit. These examples define depression.

Many people experience depression. As a teen due to hormones levels fluctuation I suffered from depression. Many people suffer from seasonal depression. It requires them to make the most of the daylight hours to maintain a stable mood. Whenever sickness takes hold, depression is often near to me. However, recently someone gave me flowers which lifted my mood and encouraged me.

Proverbs. 12:25 Heaviness in the heart of man maketh it stoop but a good word maketh it glad.

Three tips:

1.   Take a shower.
2.   Open your curtains.
3.   Take a walk outside.

What works to lift your mood? Hot shower? Journaling? Comfort food? Pen the curtains.

_____

_____

_____

_____

_____

_____

_____

_____

_____

_____

_____

_____

_____

REFINEMENT REVIEW
PROCESS

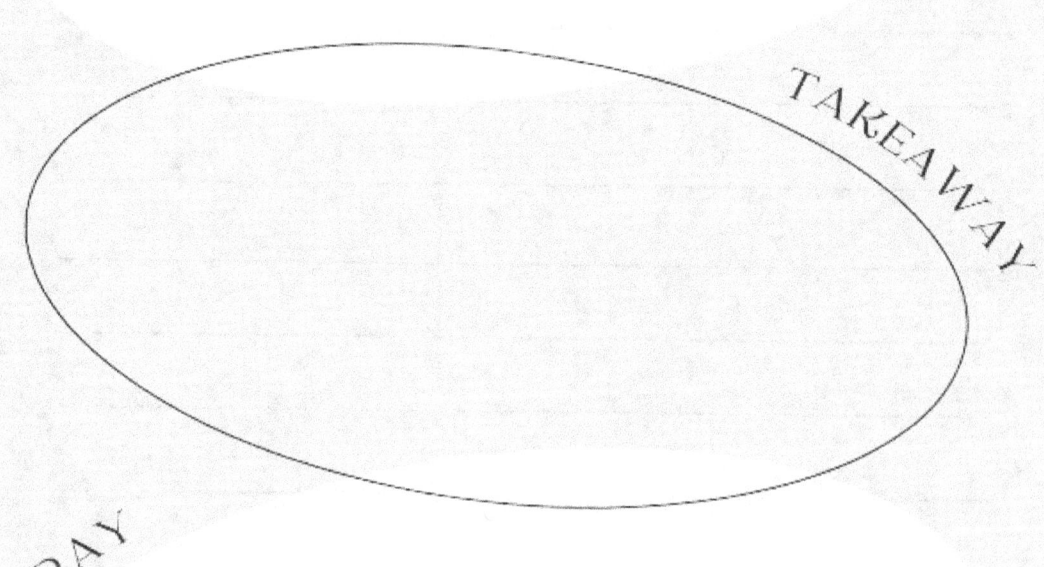

REVIEW

TAKEAWAY

PRAY

Day 11

FOCUS

A point of concentration where attention is directed. Focus is important for any goal. As a child, I often only paid attention to one thing at a time. The doctor called it singularly focused. In the world of business, "they" encourage us to multi-task. This is a divided focus.

Matthew. 6:21 For where your treasure is, there will your heart be as well."

The thing you value is the thing you will direct attention to. Is your "focus" toward the change in love you want to make? Take a moment to evaluate and refocus on that today.

Three tips:

1.   Write out a goal.
2.   Map out the steps to attain the goal.
3.   Stay focused.

What are things you need to be focused on?

_____

_____

_____

_____

_____

_____

_____

_____

_____

_____

_____

_____

_____

REFINEMENT REVIEW
PROCESS

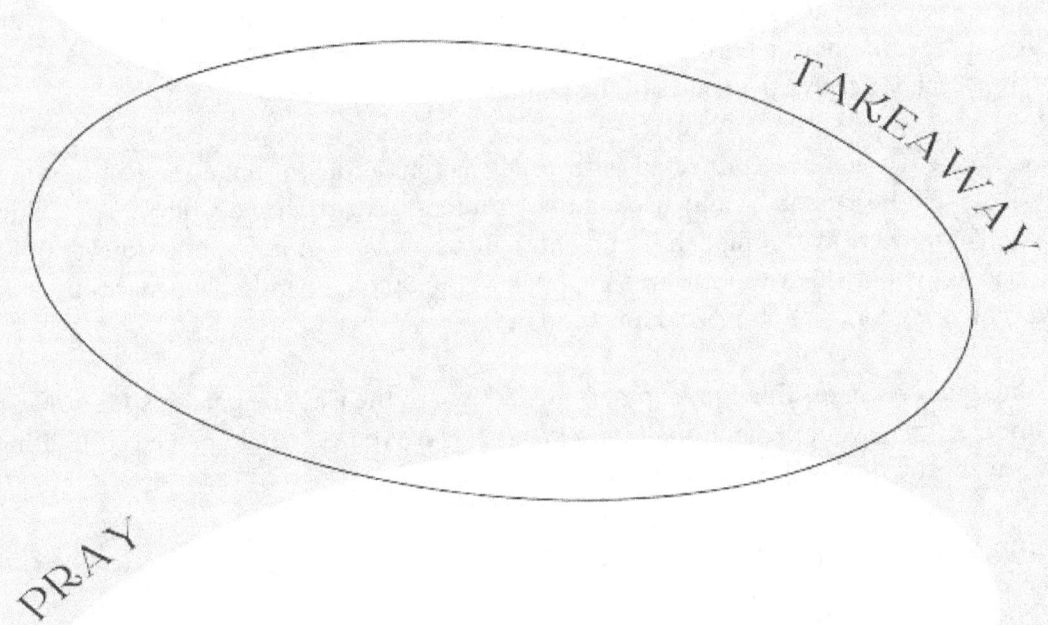

REVIEW

TAKEAWAY

PRAY

Day 12

GASLIGHTING

This is a psychological manipulation of a person usually over an extended period. That causes the victim to question the validity of their own thoughts. His or her perceptions of reality or memories and typically will lead to confusion. Which causes a loss of confidence and self esteem, uncertainty of one's emotional or mental stability, and a dependency on the perpetrator."

Roman. 16:17-18 "Now I beseech you, brethren, mark them which cause divisions and offences contrary to the doctrine which ye have learned; and avoid them. For they that are such serve not our Lord Jesus Christ, but their own belly; and by good words and fair speeches deceive the hearts of the simple."

Someone, I was once connected with used manipulation to make me feel less than adequate. The person would use subtle comments. An example would be, "I didn't realize you were as accomplished and educated as you are." A man I once knew said," If I had known my life wasn't going to happen as I planned, I would have married you." I am no one's consolation prize. I am enough.

The signs are there. This can be pinpointed, down to the way the person speaks. Never underestimate your perception. It is everything. Have you ever experienced gaslighting? How do you deal with someone that does this?

Three tips:

1.   Pay attention.
2.   Listen
3.   Set boundaries.

How have you been gaslighted in the past? How did you handle it?

_____

_____

_____

_____

_____

_____

_____

_____

_____

_____

_____

_____

_____

REFINEMENT REVIEW
PROCESS

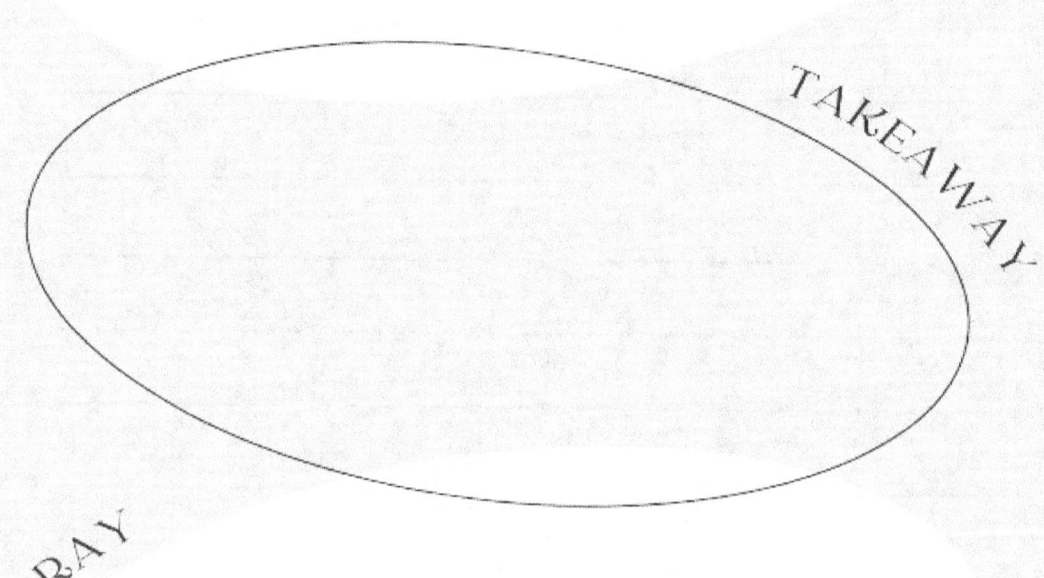

REVIEW

TAKEAWAY

PRAY

Day 13

GRIEF

The deep, poignant distress caused by bereavement. In, May 2022 my father took sick. He passed away at the end of June. This grief thing is wild. You can feel the love of the person, have an emotional reaction, and realize that the person is no longer in the space they once held. I miss my father. Loss brings grief.

Lamentations. 3:32 But though he cause grief, yet will he have compassion according to the multitude of his mercies.

Three tips:

1. Take it one day at a time.
2. Share memories of the person with someone that loved them too.
3. Sometimes emotions of grief can come inappropriately. Find a place of safety and deal with them.

In facing grief, what mechanisms can bring someone out of grief? If you experienced grief, how did you come out?

_____

_____

_____

_____

_____

_____

_____

_____

_____

_____

_____

_____

_____

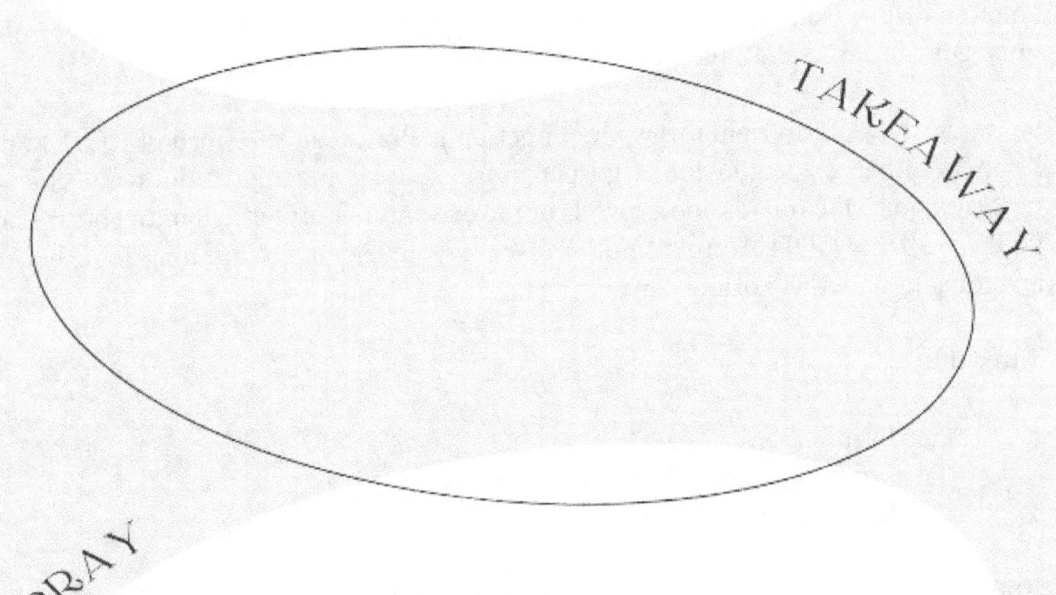

REVIEW

TAKEAWAY

PRAY

Day 14

GUT CHECK

Every day I face myself in the mirror to make an assessment of my character, to get courage, and determine how to face the day. It is necessary to gut check myself in situations of stress. I am a woman of God. I don't pretend to be anything else. I have moments when my crazy wants to act out.

The reason I say my gut check my crazy because in God I am stable. I am smart, intelligent; I am chosen; I am loved. I am all the things that GOD says I am. However, on days I wake up, on the wrong side of the bed or in a"bad mood", having a negative emotion or just feeling out of sorts. Maybe feeling like I want to say something flip. I must gut check myself in the mirror.

So, what I have to do right away when I get up is Pray, read the word of GOD, and I listen to either the audio bible, gospel music. But, if my mood does not change quickly. I go to the mirror, look myself in the eye and tell myself…Randi, you are not going to shame GOD. You will not embarrass yourself or do anything foolish. You are going to have a victorious day.

Three tips:

1.   Step back.
2.   Take a moment to think about your actions.
3.   Call for guidance before you respond.

The takeaway is, sometimes you must gut check your crazy.

What are the times when you followed your gut that it worked in your favor?

_____

_____

_____

_____

_____

_____

_____

_____

_____

_____

_____

_____

_____

REVIEW

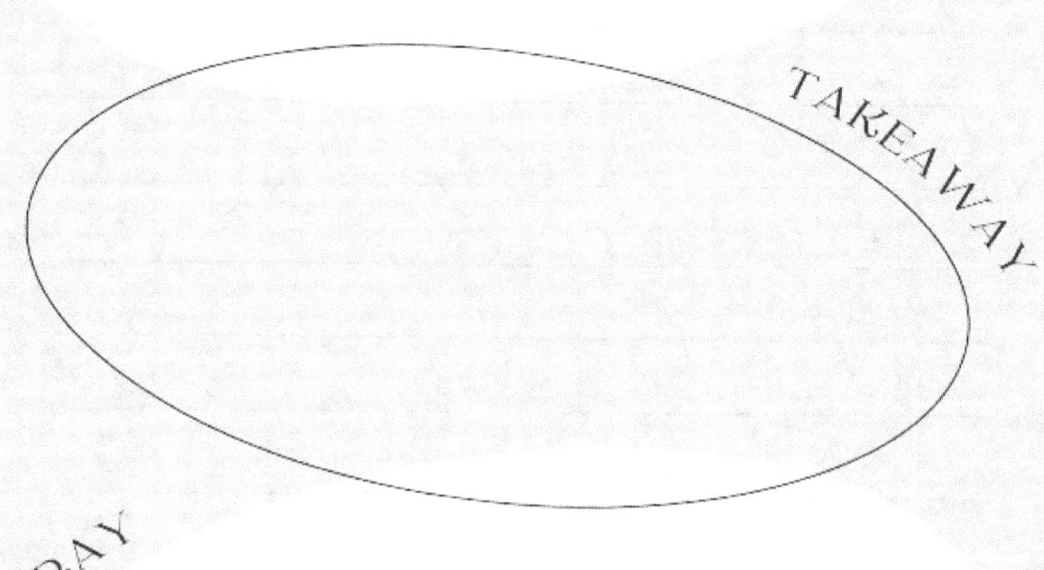

TAKEAWAY

PRAY

Day 15

SELF-CARE

Taking care of oneself is the essence of self-care. It is imperative to make time for refreshing the body, spirit, and mind. I am a caregiver. I am a mother, daughter, grandmother, sister, and friend. It has been ingrained in me from the time I was 8 years old. It taught me to look out for those I love and avow myself to. Many times in my life, I have done so at the expense of my wellbeing.

Self care is important as a caregiver, because it is so easy to take care of everyone else and forget about us. Self care is more than pampering. It is overall health. Are you saving by paying yourself every month? Getting your teeth checked and cleaned at least once a year. Having a basic physical once a year. Let's talk about taking medicines as prescribed. What about talking to a therapist when you are struggling with the cares of life? Finding a place of worship, or peace to get in touch with God's instruction for overall health.

3 John 1:2 "Beloved, I wish above all things that thou mayest prosper and be in health, even as thy soul prospereth."

Three tips:

1. Use a calendar to schedule appointments.
2. Make small changes to improve yourself, like drink more water.
3. Give yourself the same treatment you give to others as a caregiver.

What do you do to take care of self?

_____

_____

_____

_____

_____

_____

_____

_____

_____

_____

_____

_____

_____

REVIEW

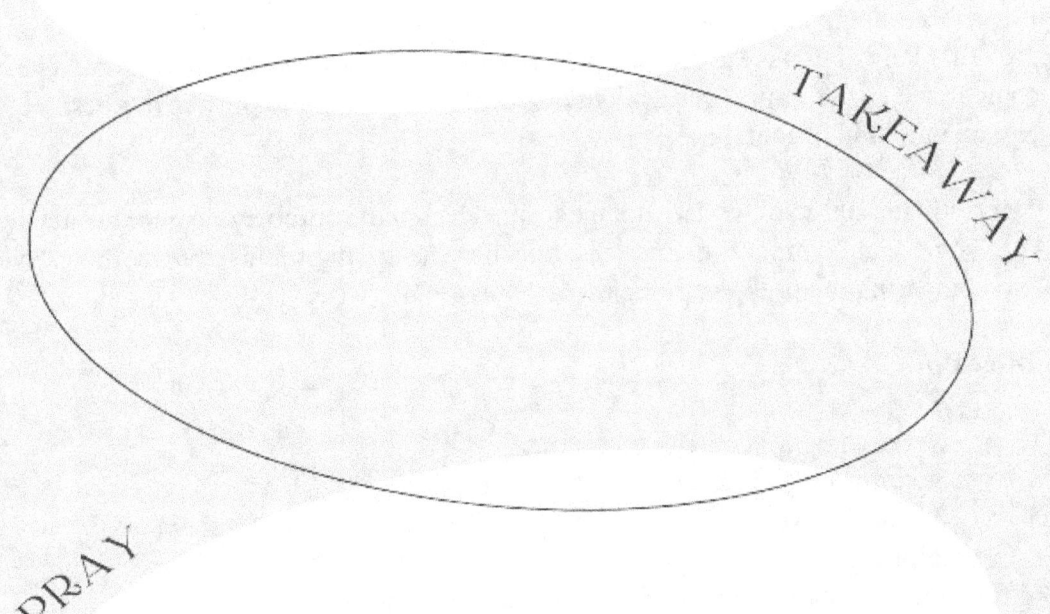

TAKEAWAY

PRAY

Day 16

SELF-SABOTAGE

Criticism of oneself with behaviors leading to one's own failure. As an adult, I still hear the words of some people telling me I am not good enough. Every event that requires my hand in it would have me questioning myself. I have found it n the last few years whenever I am criticized. The eight-year-old in my subconscious shows up. I had to realize that what I heard in my head was not always what they said. I practice asking, what I heard you say is? Sometimes it works and sometimes I must elaborate.

I had to realize there were times I was stuck. It took my trusting in God to get unstuck. I have been doing better, but there are times. I have previously hindered myself from growth. Many of us have grown up with comparisons to others. It is necessary to never compare. Each of our paths and talents are different. We should only be our best selves. Not an imitation of someone else.

2 Corinthians 10:12 For we dare not make ourselves of the number or compare ourselves with some that commend themselves: but they measuring themselves by themselves, and comparing themselves among themselves, are not wise.

Three tips:

1. Never compare yourself to another.
2. Keep running your race. Don't give up.
3. Be aware of your behaviors, and practice working through them to improve.

Often time self sabotage comes from comparing ourselves to others.

Do you recognize when you go into self-sabotage mode?
How do you rectify it?

_____

_____

_____

_____

_____

_____

_____

_____

_____

_____

_____

_____

_____

REVIEW

TAKEAWAY

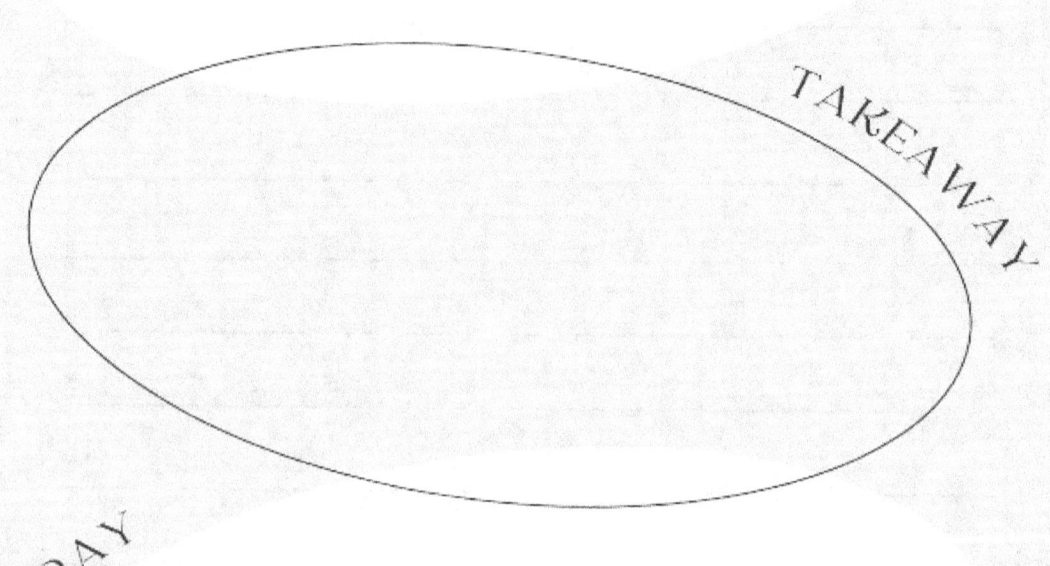

PRAY

Part 3
Physical Refinement:

Psalms 94:19- In the Multitude of my thoughts within me, Thy comforts delight my soul.

Day 17

AGING

The advancement of years gives us the ability to reflect. Yet aging is a process one should prepare for. Building blocks of life start at conception and are fortified in the first five years of life. I remember my mom giving us vitamins in the morning and juice with cod liver oil blended in. My mother fed us green vegetables and baked meals. In our home could have anything but we're not allowed to over indulge. We had to go outside and get exercise. I realize as an adult, the same rules apply. Take care of your mind, body and spirit and it will take care of you.

I was asked once when was I going to mellow out." In most cases people become more relaxed with age. I have been "old" since I was a child. I have not always followed the vitamins, exercise and eating right idea. Now, I see the importance of it. So, I am doing better.

Titus2:2 "That the aged men be sober, grave, temperate, sound in faith, in charity, in patience.

Three tips:

1. Consult your doctor.
2. Start a regime that you can live with, no fad diets.
3. Get an accountability buddy.

How do you prepare for aging? Vitamins? Vegetables? Exercise?

_____

_____

_____

_____

_____

_____

_____

_____

_____

_____

_____

_____

_____

REFINEMENT REVIEW
PROCESS

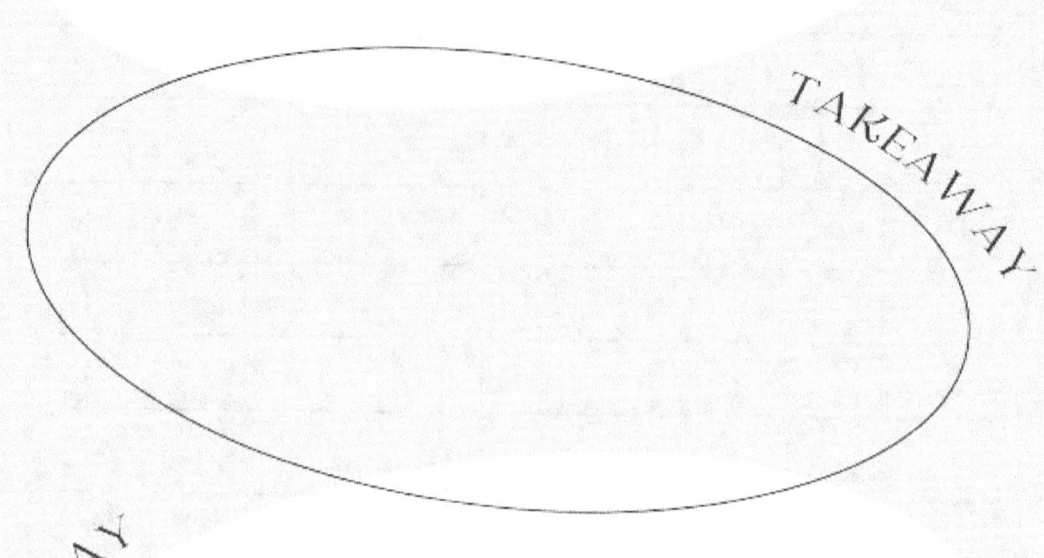

REVIEW

TAKEAWAY

PRAY

Day 18

HUNGER

I have had a strong desire, and or craving for many things. As a new believer, I had a strong desire to be like the other people in my ministry.

Luke 6:21 "Blessed are ye that hunger now: for ye shall be filled. Blessed are ye that weep now: for ye shall laugh."

As life happens at various times, there will be a strong desire for change. Not everyone has this. However, when this desire happens, the only thing that can fill it is love. For years, I struggled to look at people, circumstances, and other things. Finally, love gave me joy and has changed my appetite.

Three tips:

1. Know that desire fades, timing is everything.
2. Step out by faith.
3. Do the things that satisfy your hunger, that also is done with love.

What do you hunger for? What steps have you impltemented to achieve what you desire?

_____

_____

_____

_____

_____

_____

_____

_____

_____

_____

_____

_____

_____

_____

REFINEMENT REVIEW
PROCESS

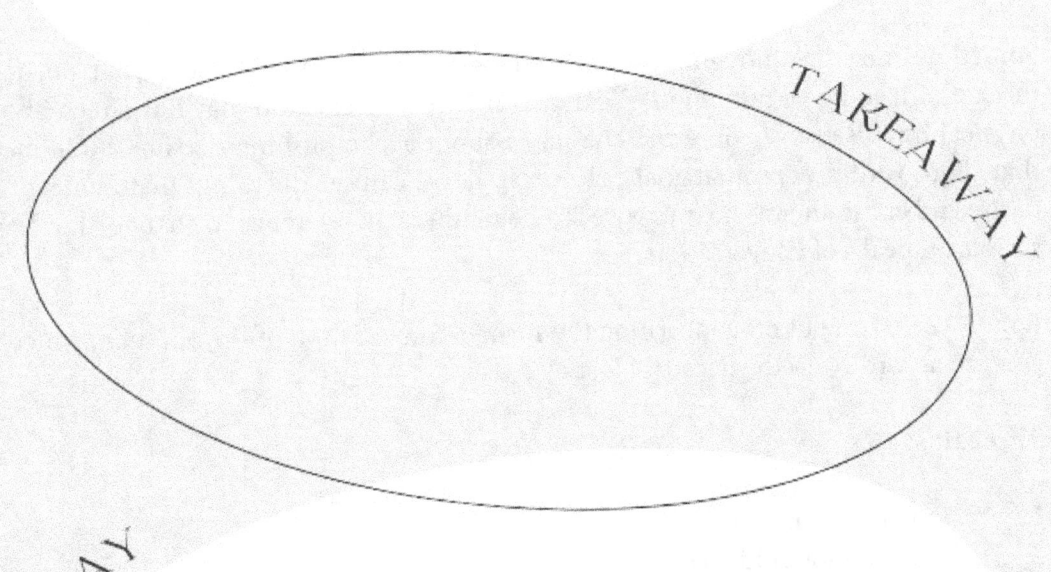

REVIEW

TAKEAWAY

PRAY

Day 19

LUST

This psychological state of an intense desire for an object, person and or thing. At various times in my life I desired a man, sex, money, or a thing. This used to be a way of life. The conversation about desires, no motivation. No movement forward.

What/who are you listening to? Many times, in the past, negative self-talk keeps success from happening. This cultivates negative habits and feelings of self-loathing. That caused me to give in to sexual pressures from men. Seeking to fulfill desires that were self-destructive, like alcohol misuse.

Sometimes negative thoughts lead to desires that take you away from your purpose instead of leading to fulfilling it. Years before the conversation may have been about physical impulses, over time the change is about accomplishing personal fulfillment that aligns with my spiritual goals. However, now I can see the things that I am lent to desire and chase after as my purpose. To help others. In reference to change, the above scripture speaks of conversation.

Eph. 5:22 that ye put off concerning the former conversation of the old man, which is corrupt according to the deceitful lusts.

Three tips:

1.   Pray for a purpose.
2.   Ask God for guidance.
3.   Write it down, hold on to the plan.

What changes in conversation have you made in order to direct lust to make changes?

_____

_____

_____

_____

_____

_____

_____

_____

_____

_____

_____

_____

_____

_____

REFINEMENT REVIEW
PROCESS

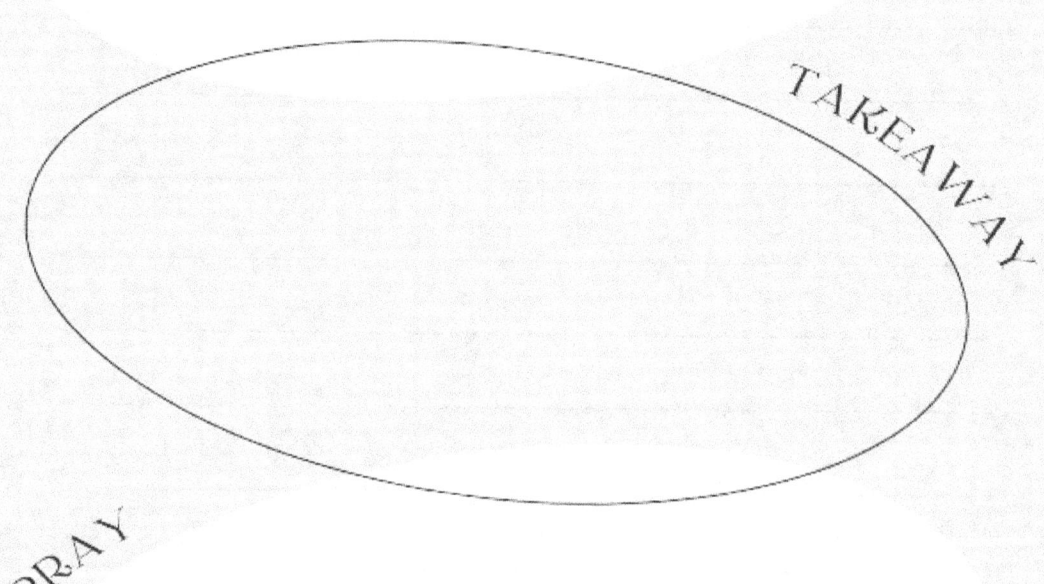

REVIEW

TAKEAWAY

PRAY

Day 20

Pain

Discomfort or uncomfortable sensation of physical, emotional or spiritual distress.

He is chastened also with pain upon his bed, and the multitude of his bones with string pain. Job 33:19

Pain can trigger many responses. When I learned about my chronic illness and began to suffer excruciating pain I responded in inappropriate ways. I feared death and wasn't coping well. As the years have gone by I have learned pain can teach you how to grow in ways being healthy never could. I've learned to move past my pain to over come any obstacle set in my way. Now, I just allow God's love to work through me. I have learned to quiet myself, take a deep breath, and let go.

Three tips:

1. Pain can be a motivator for change, how do you
    cope with pain?
2. Step backdon't allow your emotions or
    frustration to control you.
3. Listen to music, read, or pray.

What have you learned from instances of pain?

_____

_____

_____

_____

_____

_____

_____

_____

_____

_____

_____

_____

_____

_____

REVIEW

TAKEAWAY

PRAY

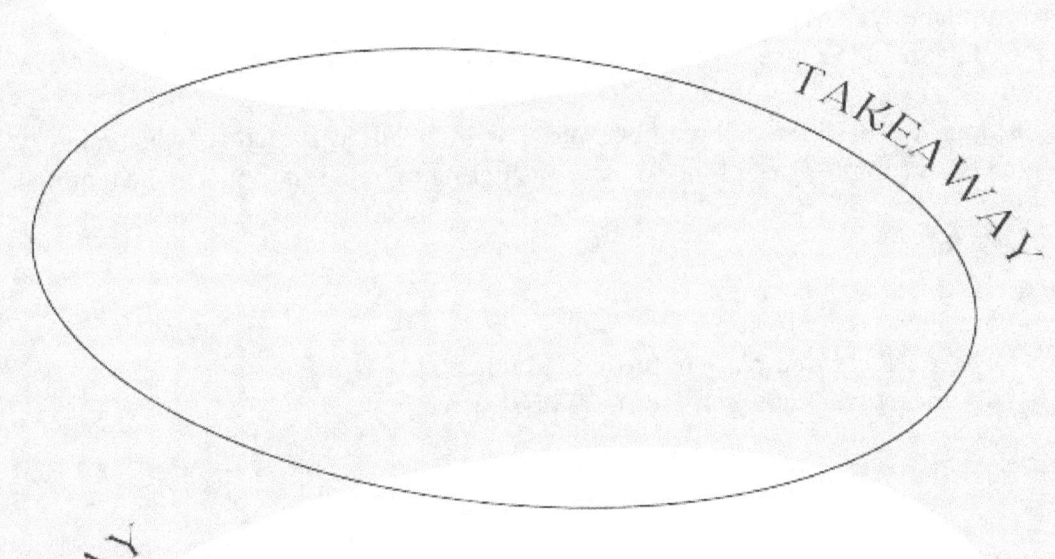

Day 21

ACCOUNTABILITY

The obligation or willingness to accept responsibility or to give an account for one's actions. There are times when as a natural person someone cannot take responsibility for their words or actions. They are not accountable. For years I was not mentally, emotionally and spiritually able to be accountable in many areas in life. As recently as a few years ago I had trouble facing myself in weakness.

The way I overcame is the scripture below. I asked for GOD to guide my heart and give my tongue the answer to everything that requires me to face responsibility and accountability. Love will make you accountable to the people you avow yourself to by blood, faith and or love. What makes you accountable?

Galatians 6:1 Brethren, if a man be overtaken in a fault, ye which are spiritual, restore such an one in the spirit of meekness; considering thyself, lest thou also be tempted.

Three tips:

1. Love allows for correction.
2. Love considers your place in the lives of others.
3. Love makes you know you are not always correct.

What have you put in place to hold yourself accountable? Do you use any tools? Is there a person you check in with?

_____

_____

_____

_____

_____

_____

_____

_____

_____

_____

_____

_____

_____

_____

PROCESS

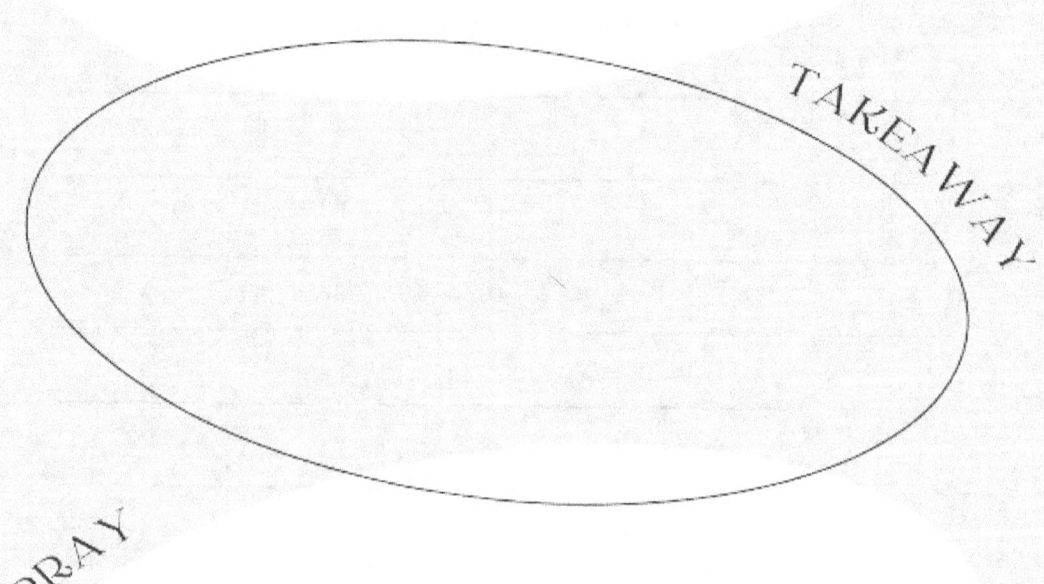

REVIEW

TAKEAWAY

PRAY

Day 22

ATTITUDE

The disposition of the body is based on how you feel. A mental position regarding a state or fact (Pose/posture).

Colossians 3:12   Put on therefore, as the elect of God, holy and beloved, bowels of mercies, kindness, humbleness of mind, meekness, long-suffering.

My topic is attitude. In so many situations and circumstances in the world we all have different attitudes. Examples of such are grateful, laid back, disgruntled and anger. An attitude of gratitude leads to a posture of instead of Why me, you will feel Why not me. Keep an attitude of gratitude and that always makes room for more.

Three tips

1. Name what you are grateful for.
2. Say Thank you and
3. Tell people that you appreciate them.

How do you keep track of your gratitude? Do you start in the morning? and do you also speak them at night?

_____

_____

_____

_____

_____

_____

_____

_____

_____

_____

_____

_____

_____

_____

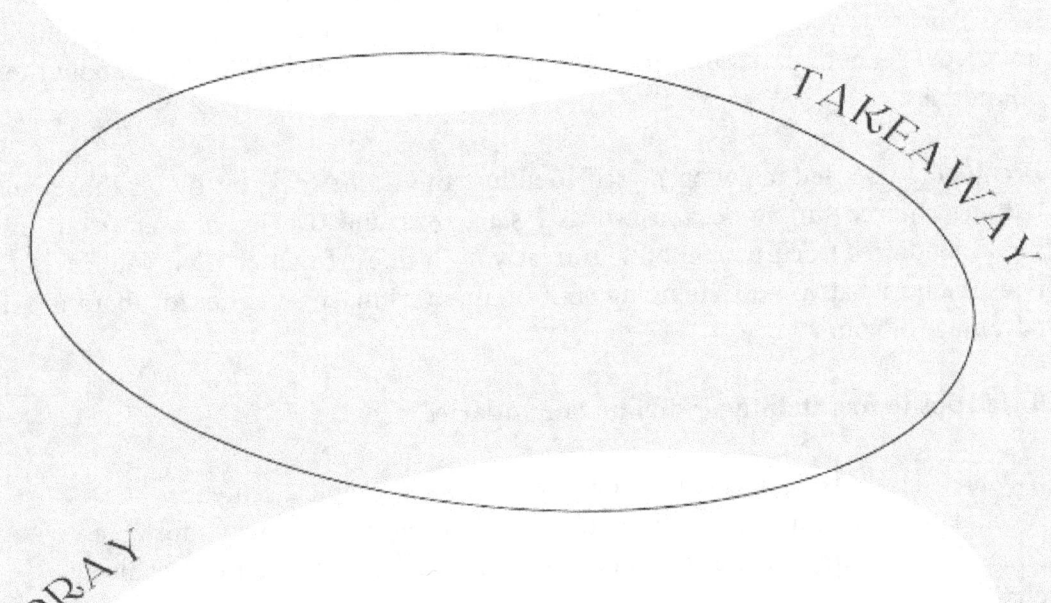

REVIEW

TAKEAWAY

PRAY

Day 23

BOUNDARIES

The defined mark or basis that sets as a limit or standard. "When the enemy shall come in like a flood, the Spirit of the Lord shall lift up a standard against him." Isaiah59:18 -KJV

When talking about boundaries, one thing that you have to start and know about yourself as an individual is where your boundaries lie. People can often say what they have as a boundary, but it does not become defined until one has to stand up for it. Some people will test those boundaries. An example of this from a personal perspective is. When I was younger and friends with a man that I was previously romantically involved; I set boundaries for him. He began to go back and forth with me about those boundaries.

Eventually, I started allowing myself to adjust the framework, bit by bit those rules I didn't enforce simply became words I sang over and over as he walked all over me. Boundaries teach people how to treat you. It doesn't matter what you say but it does matter what you do, changing your boundaries makes it easier for them to take advantage of you.

Three tips to maintaining individual boundaries.

1. When a limit is set, it is not up for debate. No is a complete sentence.
2. Values are individual, not a group project- do what makes you comfortable.
3. Take time to practice the word no, if you can't say "no" boundaries will always change.

How do deal with setting boundaries:

_____

_____

_____

_____

_____

_____

_____

_____

_____

_____

_____

_____

_____

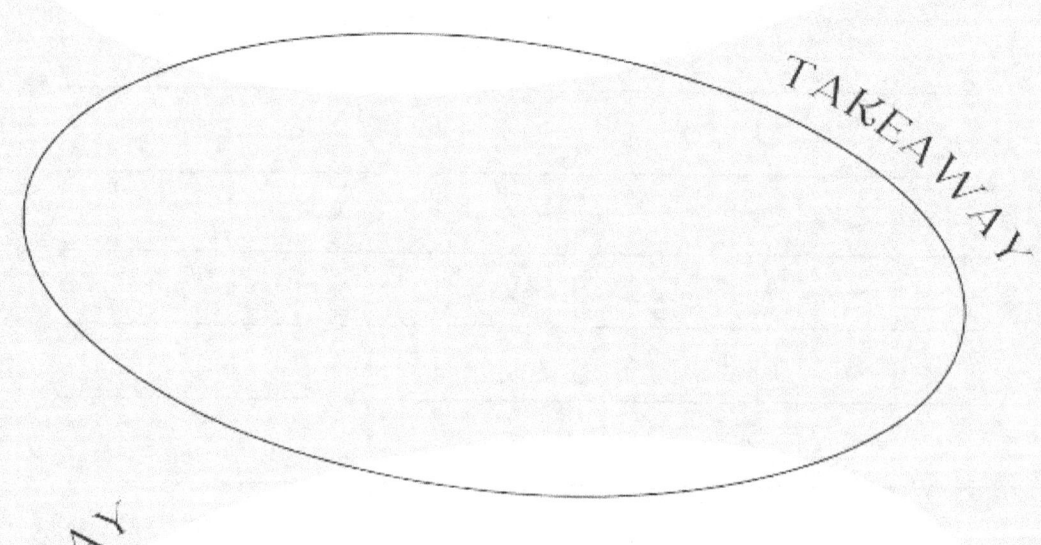

REVIEW

TAKEAWAY

PRAY

Day 24

CONFIRMATION

The state of corroborating, and or verifying (to check).
Job 20:3 I have heard the check of my reproach, and the spirit of my understanding causeth me to answer.

Confirmation: When you have received instruction in a classroom, you have received a word from the Lord. When someone says something to you. You will always receive confirmation. When dealing with science, something that's factual confirmation will always come from a different source. In spiritual matters, there is always a scientific fact, historical record, and the bible to confirm it.

Whenever you find anything that's written, there is always a source to verify where the information comes from. I would encourage you that when you are going through something, someone tells you something, you need advice for something or study something there is always a confirmation. Some might say, follow your first mind, there is always a confirmation after that. There's always confirmation when dealing with the truth. Keep that in mind, when it is true, confirmation will always follow. Some will say it's true with them, and it is not. Reference: Ezekiel 13:6

Three tips:

1.   Do not rush.
2.   Take some time.
3.   Write down everything that aligns with verification you
     are moving in the right direction.

NEED A CONFIRMATION QUESTION

_____

_____

_____

_____

_____

_____

_____

_____

_____

_____

_____

_____

_____

_____

REFINEMENT REVIEW
PROCESS

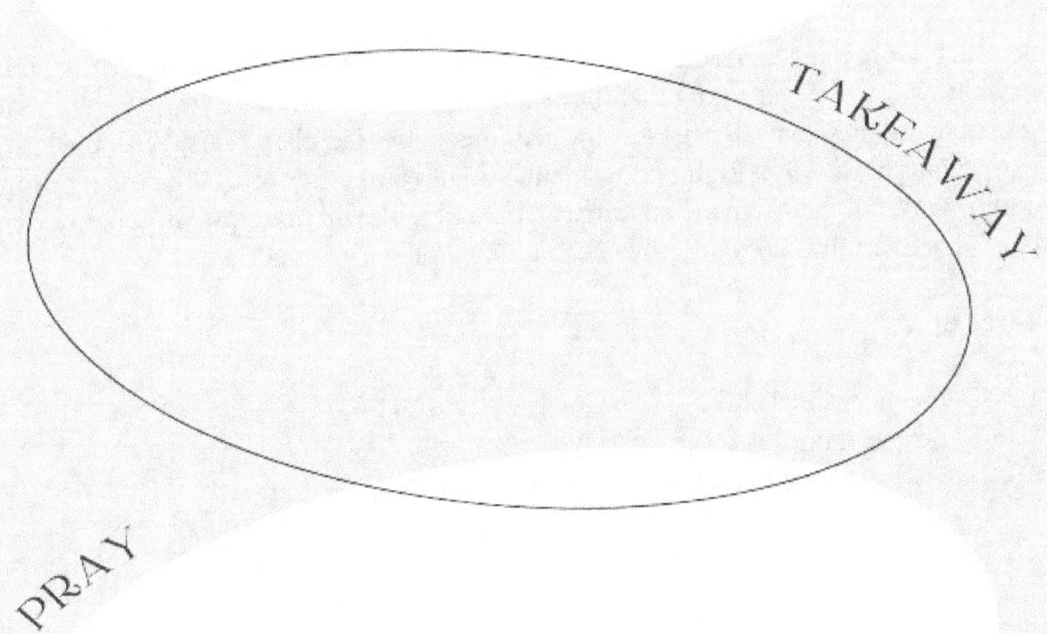

REVIEW

TAKEAWAY

PRAY

Day 25

FAITH

The expectation and strong belief in God without tangible proof. Hebrews 11.1 Now faith is the substance of things hoped for, the evidence of things not seen.

Faith, for many of us, we say that we have faith. According to the word of God, faith is the substance of things hoped for and the evidence of things not seen. With all the unrest, COVID-19 and the economy I, along with many, have been struggling with is my faith. I believe God; I believe that things are going to turn around. I believe in love; I believe in hope because without hope you will not face the trial of every day.

So much more than ever before I hear people say they just want to give up, they want to walk away from everything that they said they believed in. Recently, someone spoke to me saying these have been a few tremendously stressed filled years. With the loss of many icons of the Civil Rights Movement, athletes and other things that many people admired. Words from a man can impart faith, but faith will not grow without hope and God's Love. Faith is not faith, if you can touch it or see it.

Three tips:

1. Practice your Faith
2. Believe it until it happens
3. Listen to spiritual music, read God's word, and pray

What are some verses on faith that help you through challenging times?

_____

_____

_____

_____

_____

_____

_____

_____

_____

_____

_____

_____

_____

_____

PROCESS

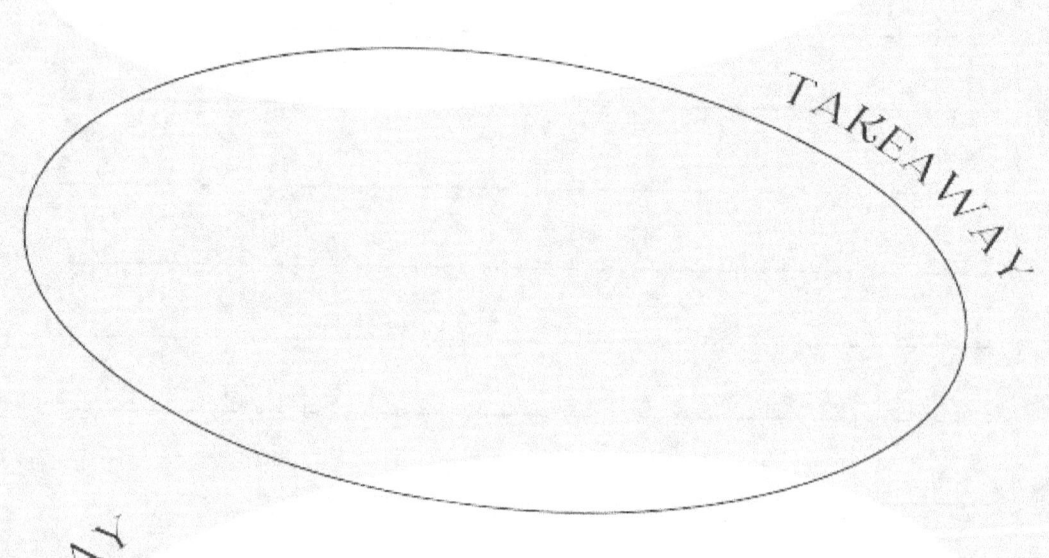

REVIEW

TAKEAWAY

PRAY

Day 26

AFFIRMATION

The assertion and recognition of the existence and value of one's individual self." Ephesians 2:4 But God, who is rich in mercy, for his great love wherewith he loved us, Ephesians 3:19-20 and to know the love of Christ, which passeth knowledge, that ye might be filled with all the fulness of God. Now unto him that is able to do exceedingly abundantly above all that we ask or think, according to the power that worketh in us,

In the past I have struggled with being strong in the grace that GOD has afforded me through the precious redeeming blood of Jesus Christ. Right before the pandemic in the fall of 2019, I had anxiety. God gave me an affirmation that I use. I say it every day, no. However, it is taped to my monitor at my desk in my home office and the desk at my work site. It affirms the woman I am in Christ Jesus. I use it as a tool to strengthen my will, encourage my heart, stand on God's promises and embrace his lovingkindness.

Tips:

1. The person speaking it must believe in the affirmation.
2. It must be spoken positively.
3. An affirmation must be used for love. (Of self, of mankind, and to God.)

My daily affirmation …

.

I am chosen. I am disciplined.
I am Free. I am Gifted.
I am loved.
I am Precious. I am powerful.
I am redeemed.
I am Talented.
I am Valued. I am wise.
I am Sanctified., I am submitted.   I am all of these by faith in Christ Jesus, my Lord..

Write your daily affirmations.

_____

_____

_____

_____

_____

_____

_____

_____

_____

_____

_____

_____

_____

REFINEMENT REVIEW
PROCESS

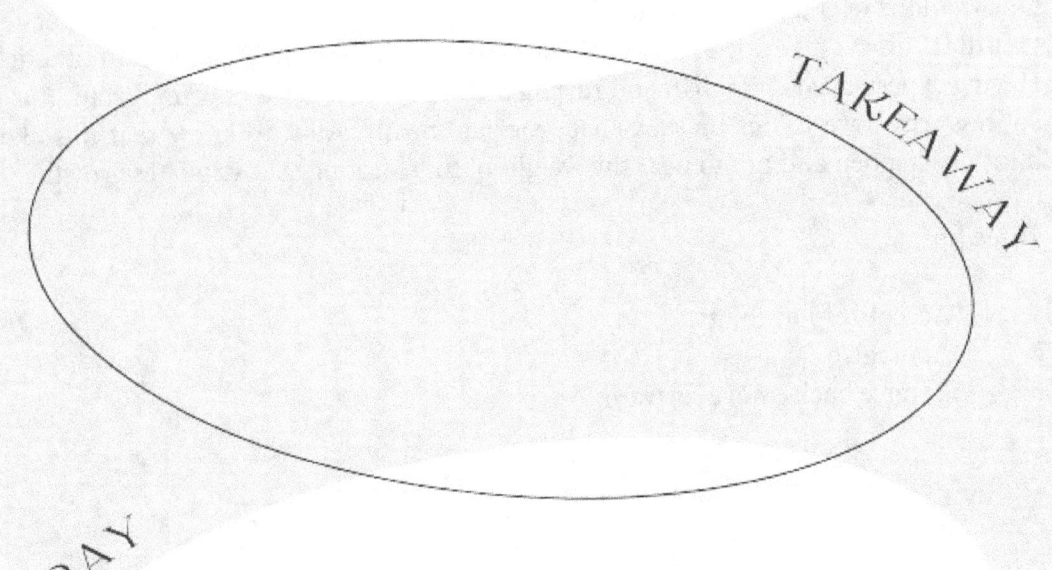

REVIEW

TAKEAWAY

PRAY

Day 27

MISTAKES

An action or judgment that is misguided or wrong.

2 Tim. 3:16 All scripture is given by inspiration of God, and is profitable for doctrine, for reproof, for correction, for instruction in righteousness:

As a child, we learn through mistakes or messes. Even into adulthood, there are times we make mistakes as individuals. As a child, your parents chastised you if I had warned you not to do something and you did it. Love works this way.

One wouldn't tell their child not to play in the street and not give them a consequence if they did it, anyway. To not do so could result in the child facing a life and death situation. Having experienced childbirth and raising a child I understand how important it is to address with love things that are inappropriate firmly. Also, to know that mistakes/ mess ups happen and not to near the weight of this for long as it stagnates growth.

Three tips:

1.   Accept responsibility.
2.   Apologize
3.   Bounce back- move forward.

How do you deal with mistakes?

_____

_____

_____

_____

_____

_____

_____

_____

_____

_____

_____

_____

_____

REFINEMENT REVIEW
PROCESS

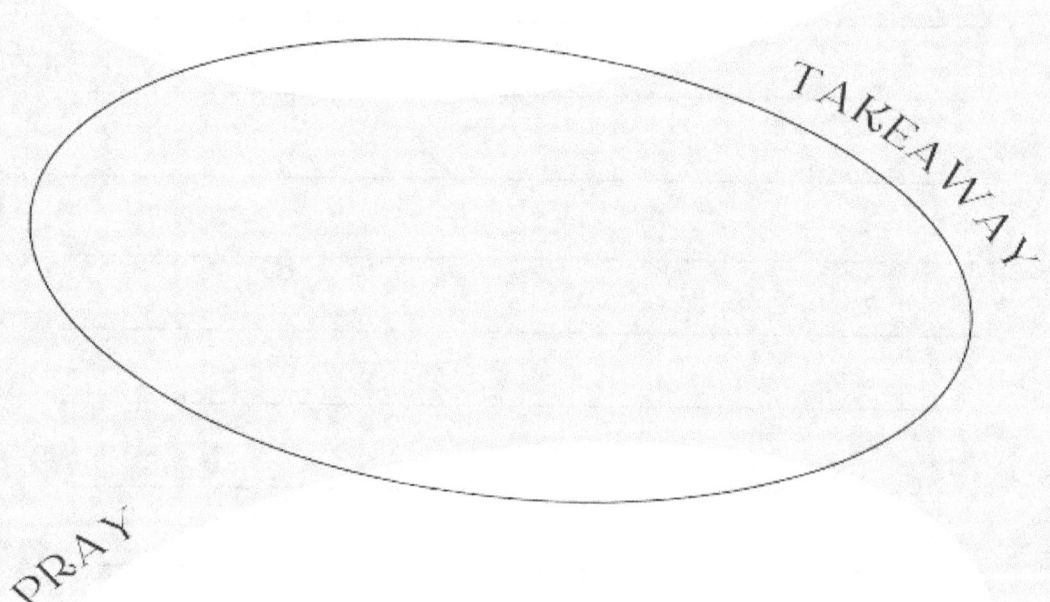

REVIEW

TAKEAWAY

PRAY

Day 28

PEOPLE-PLEASING

Gal.4:10 For do I now persuade men or God? Or do I seek to please men? For if I yet please men, I should not be the servant of Christ.

People pleasers are defined as a person that has an emotional need to please others even at the expense of their own needs or desire.

Whenever someone has suffered abuse, or any other traumatic event early in life before a certain age they will most assuredly suffer from either an identity crisis or they will be people pleasers. In more recent days, I have learned to be more in sync with my feelings and emotions. For years, I had not learned to say no. I would say yes even in situations that were uncomfortable or unpleasant to me. During the last few years, the intent was to be self-examining. In doing so, I realized that from a child I was always doing things I didn't want to do. To that end it is not selfless if helping someone hurts you. Is there a daily struggle with saying No. Yes, there is.

Three tips:

1. Practice saying No.
2. Write down guidelines to follow, boundaries.
3. Journal.

Do you find yourself over extended and struggling with saying no? How do you stop?

_____

_____

_____

_____

_____

_____

_____

_____

_____

_____

_____

_____

_____

_____

REFINEMENT REVIEW
PROCESS

REVIEW

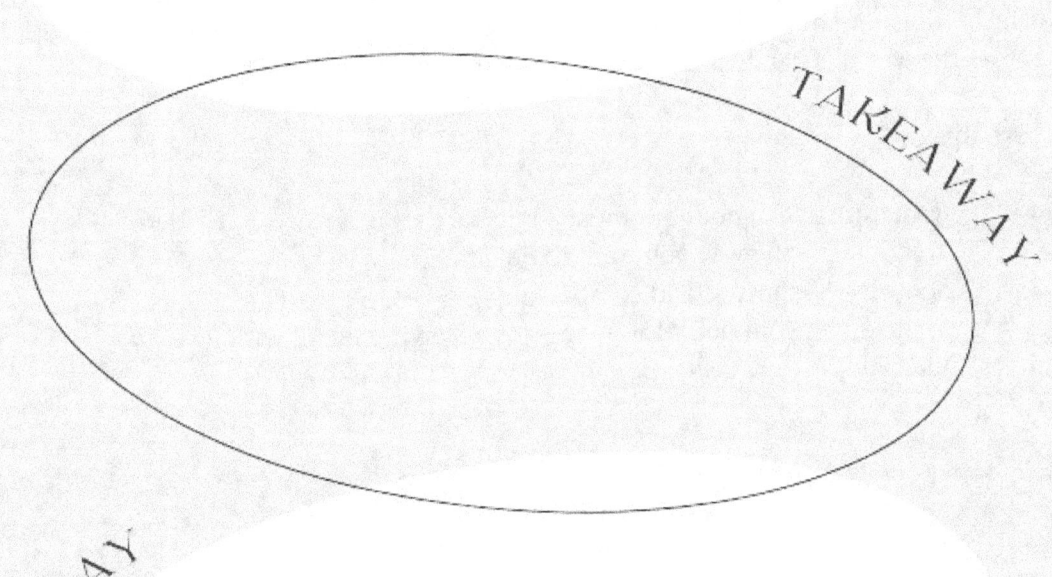

TAKEAWAY

PRAY

Day 29

REAPING WHAT YOU SOW

(Galatians.6:7 Be not deceived; God is not mocked: for whatsoever a man soweth, that shall he also reap.)- Sow defined as" to set in motion or spread abroad. Reap is defined as "to gather."

Have you ever had a dreadful week, month, year? There will be times when things will work out, and there will be times that will be rough or easy. When I was younger, my mother used to say, "what goes around comes around". Keep in mind, some people think they can treat people any kind of way and everything will work out. No. That which you sow, you shall also reap. Whatever you put out will come back to you. Be mean, the world is harsh. Show love and it will always come back to you.

Five tips:

1. Remember what goes out must come back in
2. Treat people the way you want to be treated
3. Show love, kindness and compassion
4. Write down your goals for giving and receiving. Do it with love.
5. Journal

What have you sown? Do you sow love? Do you sow goodness?
Whatever you sow, will come back to you.

_____

_____

_____

_____

_____

_____

_____

_____

_____

_____

_____

_____

_____

REFINEMENT REVIEW
PROCESS

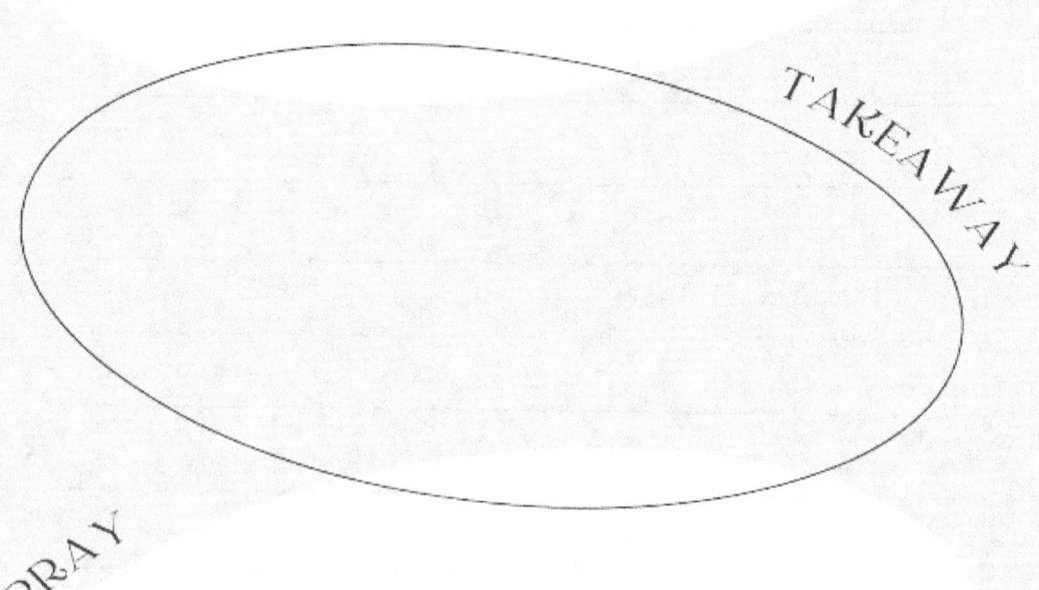

REVIEW

TAKEAWAY

PRAY

Day 30

CONTENTMENT / COMPARISON

Heb.13:5b- and be content with such things as ye have)- Content defined as "satisfied, or appeased desires."- Comparison defined as "the denotation of the differences of quality, quantity and or relation to."

Many times, in life, we stumble over ourselves. We do this because we compare ourselves to others. When we compare ourselves to others, we become discontented. This opens the door to envy, depression, lust, etc. It wasn't until I allowed myself to be content with the things; I had that I began to not envy others for their cars, man, or job.

Five Tips:

1. When you wake up start your day in gratitude.
2. Comparison is an enemy of hope, it steals peace.
3. Write down your goals.
4. Write ways to get to the goal.
5. Take one step at a time to reach the goal.

What do you do to find contentment?

_____

_____

_____

_____

_____

_____

_____

_____

_____

_____

_____

_____

_____

_____

REFINEMENT REVIEW
PROCESS

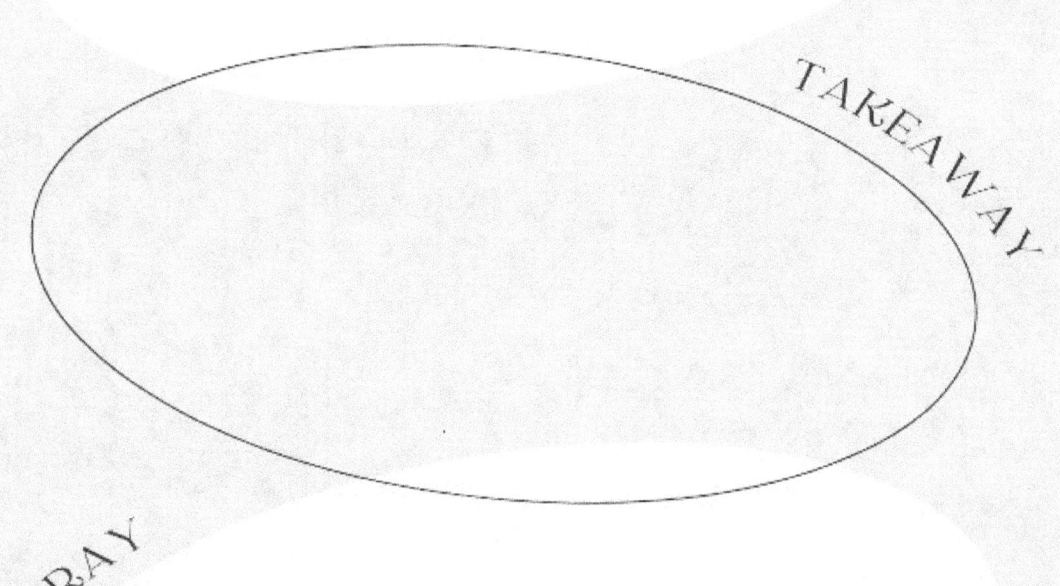

REVIEW

TAKEAWAY

PRAY

Week 1

Submission (James.4:7 Submit yourselves therefore to God. Resist the devil, and he will flee from you.)- as defined as "the act of submitting to the authority of GOD.

Three tips:

1. Submission is simply – trust of authority
2. Trust the authority you give yourself to
3. Believe that who you submit to has your best interests at heart

Week 2

Trials-(Never ask for Patience,)
James 1:3 knowing this, that the trying of your faith work eth patience.

Three tips:

1.   Don't speak in negativity.
2.   Everyone is facing something, allow grace for yourself and others.
3.   Write situations down, chronicle what you are learning from these experiences to refer to them in the future.

Week 3

COMMUNICATION

Growing up, I was taught what happens here stays here. This is the precursor to my abuser telling me, this is our little secret- don't tell anyone. These words were placed in my head and reigned deep in my spirit until I was close to fifty years old. Effective communication starts in the head of the person conveying information.

Knowing this and being able to effectively convey information takes a openness and skill few people possess. The reason for this is because most people have a natural way of thinking that is primarily rooted in self preservation. Which, leads to manipulation or purposely omitting information to keep people from knowing oneself in depth personally.

I was having a conversation with someone and realized that I was not sharing information properly with them. I was vague. It has been taught so completely to me that I have come to realize that is in my unconscious behaviors. Good communication makes for strong personal, and business relationships.

Hebrews 13:16 But to do good and to communicate forget not; for with such sacrifices GOD is well pleased.

Three tips:

1. Don't speak quickly, words have power.
2. Communicating is important in all avenues of life. It is a learned behavior.
3. Listen to your soul, it guides you into proper speaking.

End Note

When I started this journal, the intention was to write this after the mini podcast that I have been dropping topics in for over a year. During this time of writing, I became ill. I struggled with self-sabotage and became frustrated. When I reviewed the submission of this project, I realized the original submission was not only incomplete it was mangled with sentences that did not make sense. I used the voice command to write when I was under the weather and it was a hot mess on paper.

I had to get out of my own way and give myself a moment to allow God to work in his lovingkindness. I am a month past my deadline. I have another project that was born through this process. I let go of something I hoped for to get to this point. The point of this all is to deal with everything I dreamed of. Letting each thing go in order to live in the purpose for which I was intended.

Never give up your purpose for a daydream.

Randi

About Randi Coley

Born the last year of the 60's. Educated with a Bachelor's in Psychology and Maters of Health Science in Addictions studies. She is an addiction and mental counselor that has worked in the helping and social services field for twenty years. She is an entrepreneur with two community outreach organizations. Her goal through various forms of media is to educate, inspire, motivate, and uplift by words of inspiration, mentoring, leadership and behavioral modification practices for change.

Coming soon . . .

A variety of anecdotal short stories with life lessons, and salutes to those that have affected me over the course of my 50 plus years of life. That impact may have been knowledge, taught me a skill or even gut checked me. I have written about it and thanked them for this work. Gospel singer James Cleveland sang the song "Give Me My Flowers". I can't sing, so here is my offing. The words from the pen of a ready writer. Psalms 45:1.

Poetry, Prose, and words of inspiration. A collection of writings. While passing the time, sometimes I just write it down. and expound on it later. Writing is where I let my Freedom live.